Performance Management for the 21st Century: The Seismic Shift to Regular Performance Coaching

DAVID SMITH

Grosvenor House
Publishing Limited

This book is published by
Grosvenor House Publishing Ltd
Link House
140 The Broadway, Tolworth, Surrey, KT6 7HT.
www.grosvenorhousepublishing.co.uk

This book is a work of Non-fiction. Any resemblance to
people or events, past or present, is purely coincidental.

A CIP record for this book
is available from the British Library

ISBN 978-1-78623-121-5

DEDICATION

To my two sons: Simon and Mike – both of whom give me a real sense of pride and pleasure in equal measure.

1. PREAMBLE

WHY WRITE A 3rd BOOK?

> "The superior man is distressed by his lack of ability"
>
> Confucius – Chinese Philosopher

'Asda Magic' – the beginning of my story

My first book was an exploration of the turnaround of the Asda retail business after near bankruptcy in the early 1990's. Living through 15 years of cultural turnaround and change management – and seeing the resulting high performance gave me superb learning and insight.

I experienced first hand what worked, and importantly what didn't work, in order to build a high performance culture. The resulting book 'Asda Magic – the 7 principles of building a high performance culture', charts that turnaround case study. En route, it enabled Asda to become Britain's No1 Best Place to work in the Sunday Times survey.

I have been delighted by the comments I have received from readers of Asda Magic – which encouraged me to write a second book.

'Culture trumps Strategy' – the ongoing story

Following my move out of 35 years of corporate life to start my own business, I was encouraged to write a second book about what I had observed in businesses since my years at Asda. 'Culture trumps Strategy', my second book, uses my 7 principles of building a high performance culture, but the examples and stories are drawn from a variety of businesses. Some of these businesses I have worked with, some are based on CEO interviews, and some are stories I have picked up along the way. All are great exemplars of businesses seeking to build high performance cultures.

So....................why write a 3rd book?

Performance Management – the perennial 'Achilles heel' of the Leader

In my business, I run Masterclasses on a variety of subjects for clients and CEO groups. By far and away the most frequent requests from CEOs are for my Masterclass on the topic of Performance Management.

Why is this? Most CEOs openly admit that Performance Management is their greatest weakness within their organisation. Executives are aware that they avoid managing the performance issues occurring with individuals who work for them. This might be for a variety of reasons. For some, they have a close personal relationship with some colleagues. They may even have started out in the business together, but the job has outgrown their partner executive. It's extremely challenging to have a discussion about issues of underperformance with a friend and colleague with whom you socialise.

In other cases, it's more about the prospect of the sheer amount of time to be taken in performance management discussions. There are many demands on time for an Executive – many of which are both urgent and important. It is therefore all too easy to avoid a time consuming performance discussion (which we are dreading having to face into) using the excuse "I'm just too busy at the moment".

If Executives are honest, and many are brutally honest when they talk to me about this topic, they just don't like facing into conflict. That may be caused by worries about getting the procedure wrong, and subsequently being taken to an Employment Tribunal. I am staggered by how few Executives have ever been to an Employment Tribunal, yet they have this major fear of the unknown. Employment Tribunals are open to the public, and I regularly advise Executives to spend an hour of their time just sitting at the back of another employer's Employment Tribunal. It is informative and educational, and takes away the irrational fear of the unknown. It can also give an Executive the know how to avoid the pitfalls seen in the case they observe!

For some Executives, the fear of conflict is not about legal challenge, nor the potential costs/PR damage – but the interpersonal aspect of the conflict itself. Some of us hate argument; disagreement; the potential ruining of a working relationship and the ensuing 'ripples' of perceived 'damage' within the organisation. My own view is that when there is an underperformance or behavioural issue in the organisation, the workforce are usually desperate for the Executive to intervene. They are silently willing somebody in leadership to do something about the problem. Far from objecting, they will actually applaud any leader who tackles the issue.

Facing into underperfomance is not actually as hard as we first believe. More of that later in this book.

If you are an Executive who lacks skill or will in this area of performance management, then this book is for you – and let me assure you that you are by no means alone. You probably align with many fellow leaders.

Another even shorter book

My second book, 'Culture trumps Strategy' was deliberately shorter than my first book. This was due to reader feedback. Executives told me that busy people tend not to have the time to read books. They like a short and pithy read. I was told "say what you have to say – and then shut up". I think it's a worthy mantra, and I'm trying to listen to the feedback of my readers!

So here is my 3rd book – which will be shorter again than my 2nd!

2. THE FUTURE OF PERFORMANCE MANAGEMENT

2016 McKINSEY & Co REPORT : WHAT HAPPENS AFTER COMPANIES JETTISON TRADITIONAL YEAR END PERFORMANCE EVALUATIONS?

> "Performance Management isn't dead. The old way of thinking about it is." Anita Bowness
>
> "Executives owe it to the organisation, and to their fellow workers, not to tolerate non performing individuals in important jobs." Peter Drucker
>
> "Wow, I'm so excited for my performance appraisal today! (said no one............ ever)" Kevin Cruse

Ahead of the Curve – 2016 – Mckinsey & Co

I was very taken by the 2016 McKinsey report 'Ahead of the Curve', which talks about the very latest developments, indicating the potential future of performance management.

It correlates with what I am beginning to see in a variety of businesses, and what I read about from a number of sources. It's no secret, according to McKinsey research, that the yearly ritual of evaluating the performance of people in work has become one of the abiding absurdities of organisational life.

Those being appraised, and those doing the appraising find the process time consuming; often subjective; frequently demotivating and ultimately unhelpful!! According to the 2016 McKinsey report, it does little to improve the performance of employees, and more often acts as a demotivator.

None of this research conclusion is new. The latest view is that............as work has become faster moving and more fluid – so the annual ritual of performance appraisal has become more outdated as a means of managing people. McKinsey liken it to resemble conducting a modern financial transaction via carrier pigeons! I love that metaphor!!

It seems incredible, that McKinsey cite 9 out of 10 companies worldwide which are still continuing to generate annual performance scores for their employees – using them as the basis for compensation decisions. So, despite this process being viewed as out-dated, clunky, and generally derided by all – managers and companies are reluctant to change it. This is only natural. They are not sure what a re-vamped performance management system would look like. They worry that people might 'ease back' on their performance if the system changed. Moreover, they are concerned to have a fair basis for annual pay reviews to replace the process they currently undertake.

McKinsey quote companies such as G.E. and Microsoft (who both previously supported a stack and rank approach) are abandoning their annual approach to performance management, replacing it with continual feedback and coaching methods. McKinsey also report that Netflix doesn't measure its people against annual objectives – because its objectives are quite fluid, and can change rapidly.

McKinsey talk of 'Emerging Patterns' in Performance Management

There are examples of many companies collecting more objective performance data, via systems which automate 'real time' data analysis.

McKinsey research also reveals that performance data is being used less as a crude instrument for setting compensation.

A further identified trend is for companies to use fact based performance and development discussions to look forward (rather than the old fashioned backward looking annual performance appraisals).

McKinsey conjecture that these emerging patterns will play out in different ways in different companies and sectors. Despite change in pace across organisations and sectors, the bottom line is that the performance management frameworks of yesteryear need radical and seismic change in order to meet the needs of business going forward.

McKinsey's research on rethinking performance management

The outdated performance management models of today are outmoded because they date back to the work of Frederick W. Taylor in the early 1900s. Since that inception, performance management has embraced concepts such as the K.P.I.'s of the balanced scorecard, but these processes have merely served (according to McKinsey) in adding layers of complexity to a simple mechanistic principle. Companies have been trying to adapt an 'industrial era' process to ever larger and more complex modern work situations in a much faster moving world.

Managers have struggled valiantly to attempt to rate employees as best they can, using cumbersome and inaccurate information. They have been forced to adhere to distribution guidelines, which McKinsey find to be usually based around a bell shaped or normal distribution curve. Those guidelines assume that the vast majority of employees cluster around a mean, with a few over or under performing.

McKinsey contend that bell curves may not reflect reality. Their research suggests that talent and performance profiles look more like power-law distributions or Pareto curves. These resemble a hockey stick graph. One 2012 study found that the top 5% of employees outperform the average by 400%.

Google quote this particular research in influencing their own performance and talent practices. They pay top performers 500% more than average. This probably means getting rid of ratings for all but top performers. Indeed, the work of researchers Bob Sutton and Jeffrey Pfeffer have shown that it makes sense to remove ratings which demotivate and irritate employees. G.E.; the Gap and Adobe Systems have all dropped ratings systems for performance management on the back of such research. They all concentrate on building fluidity of objectives; frequent feedback discussions with individuals, and forward looking coaching discussions.

McKinsey talk about the companies who view shading minimal differentials in average performance as a 'fool's errand'. Conducting annual ratings on a bell curve model will not get more out of people, and potentially will demotivate many.

McKinsey's Summary – data which matters in performance management

Having objective data is crucial to a change in performance management processes. Employees hated the old moribund annual appraisal processes because they were subjective and based on outdated facts.

G.E. currently uses a tool called P.D.@G.E. that facilitates requests for feedback and keeps a record when received. Feedback comes online from supervisors; colleagues and other internal customers. G.E. people get regular feedback, so that they can react and readjust rapidly. The technology doesn't replace performance conversations; it merely means that your boss can chat with you regularly, using up to date observations, and coach accordingly.

McKinsey believe that automated feedback tools can remove time consuming data collection, and leave ample time for regular up to date; accurate and helpful performance coaching. To my mind, this sounds to be a really simple, practical and effective way forward for the 21st Century way of working.

Are Organisations brave enough to ditch conventional wisdom on compensation?

Conventional wisdom has always compensated employees on performance evaluation scores.

However, everyone realises that managers have always 'gamed' whatever system existed in their particular organisation. One year, they would use money from the 'pool' to look after someone who had outperformed spectacularly. The next year, that outperformer would have to endure 'taking a hit for the team' however well they subsequently performed. The 'pool' money would be used for some other person.

Evaluation systems (according to McKinsey) have traditionally bred cynicism and demotivation amongst employees..........often leading to combative discussions with their manager at pay award time.

Many companies are beginning to prefer a competitive base pay arrangement, with bonuses linked to the Company's overall performance. McKinsey feel that breaking the link between performance and compensation allows companies to worry less about tracking historical data, and more about building capability and inspiring future performance.

McKinsey quote that companies in high performing sectors, such as technology, finance and media, are 'ahead of the curve' in adapting to the future of digital work. These are the businesses pioneering the seismic transformation of performance management.

The McKinsey report urges many more companies to follow............and quickly...........and I would endorse that thought. You may read some of the statements in this Chapter as 'heresy', bearing in mind past accepted wisdom. Bear with me as you read. I hope to persuade you that there is a new and simple way forward for managing performance which has real logic and will add value.

First though, I feel we need some basic history of how and where performance management has changed.

SUMMARY POINTS :

- Are you satisfied with the performance management framework of your own business/organisation?

- Are you aware of significant seismic change to performance management in leading edge organisations?

- Are your own people highly critical of a subjective annual performance appraisal process?

- Is your annual pay award clunky, and a continual source of dissatisfaction?

YOUR ACTION :

If all or any of these questions produce the answer "yes"........then read on for the solutions!

3. THE HISTORY OF PERFORMANCE MANAGEMENT

UNDERSTAND THE PAST BEFORE RECOMMENDING A NEW FUTURE

"If you can't measure it, you can't manage it." Peter Drucker

"Although performance appraisals have been in place for generations, until recently, very little effort was given to understanding whether the process motivated employees or irritated them." Gallup

"The greatest leader is not necessarily the one who does the greatest things. He is the one who gets the other people to do the greatest things." Ronald Reagan

"When dealing with people, remember you are dealing with creatures of emotion, not logic." Dale Carnegie

---

The Changes Afoot

I am reading regularly in the business press and a variety of sources, that 65% of U.K. firms are re-thinking their performance management processes. The emerging common theme (with which I wholeheartedly concur) is that the regularity of feedback and discussion of performance is key to that changed process.

Microsoft; G.E.; Netflix; Google; Deloitte and Accenture are in the vanguard of change. They are by no means stupid businesses. This is a change to which all business leaders today should be paying attention.

Harvard Business Review published an article in October 2016, by Peter Cappelli and Anna Travis, entitled 'The Performance Management Revolution'. In it, they talk particularly about the point in the early 2000s – when abandoning the traditional appraisal process seemed to be heresy – but that since then, more than one third of U.S. companies have done exactly that. This trend began in Silicon Valley, but has swept across the U.S., with many businesses adopting frequent check-ins between managers and employees.

For me, this seismic change to an old fashioned and 'industrial age' management process is no longer just a fad.....................it is a real here to stay modern day requirement in managing the performance of people effectively.

Performance Management origins in Ford Motor Co

I have already mentioned in Chapter 2 that the thinking behind the original performance management processes began with the work of F.W.Taylor at the Model T Ford production line in the early 1900s.

By the 1940s, Cappelli and Travis found that 60% of U.S. companies were using annual performance appraisals to document worker performance and to allocate rewards.

Jack Welch and forced ranking at G.E.

By the 1980s, Jack Welch as CEO of G.E., became famous for championing forced ranking to reward top performers, accommodate those in the middle range, and to remove those at the bottom.

Interestingly, by the 2000s, as organisations began to flatten their hierarchies, it became increasingly hard to run those huge bureaucratic performance appraisal systems. There was also a growing suspicion amongst line managers, that the whole process itself was demotivational for the many under their charge. In many cases, as previously mentioned.................line managers began to 'game' those unfair clunky systems.

Willis Towers Watson and Deloitte research into performance management

Cappelli and Travis share my view that line managers hated doing reviews. That was clear from anecdotal feedback, and backed up by survey after survey. Willis Towers Watson found that typically 45% of line managers found no value whatsoever in the performance management systems they were being forced to use. Deloitte also reported their own findings, that 58% of HR executives (who were charged with designing and administering performance management processes)

.... viewed performance reviews as an ineffective use of management time!!

There is little doubt now that the re-thinking of the whole performance management process has risen to the top of many executive team agendas. Deloitte captured it succinctly in my view as "a process which invests 1.8million hours across the firm, yet doesn't fit the needs of our business." That's quite a damning statement. 1.8million hours! No wonder they changed their processes.

Why do CEOs carry on using redundant performance management processes?

It is a conundrum. Why have so many businesses, many run by go ahead CEOs, carried on with such hated performance review processes for decades? It is widely known that these processes generate mountains of box ticking/form filling paperwork – whilst restricting creativity and serving no real purpose except to justify the annual pay award ratings.

Wasn't it Einstein himself who said that to keep repeating the same process and expect a different result was the very definition of insanity? Then by Einstein's definition, traditional performance management processes are a piece of corporate insanity!!

Many employers are finally beginning to acknowledge that line managers and their subordinates despise and loathe the performance appraisal processes of yesteryear. These end of year rituals, have perennially attempted to hold people accountable for long past behaviour and results. Unfortunately, this has been at the expense of seeking to improve current performance, and to groom talent for the future.

Cappelli and Travis reckon from their research that 70% of multinational companies are moving toward designing a new model...............which emphasises regular informal conversations about performance and development – that is a real change of focus to building a high performing and competitive workforce.

'Agile Principles' : 2000 onwards

The 'Agile' trend began in 2001, when software developers created what they called the 'Agile manifesto'. Their work favoured responding to change, above doggedly following a rigid plan. 'Agile' represented principles such as collaboration; self-organisation; self-direction and regular reflection on how to work more effectively. Many sectors do not work in the 'tech bubble', but all businesses have to respond in real time to customer feedback, and the changing requirements of their market. All of which is getting ever faster.

It seems to me that though 'Agile principles' began in software companies nearly 20 years ago, those were the principles which most drove the move to a different definition of effectiveness on the job than had historically been the case. Agile principles are completely juxtaposed with the old fashioned practice of cascading goals from the top down and assessing people against them one year later.

I believe that business leaders need to ride this trend of change in performance management processes, because businesses need to be more agile in the 21st Century environment in which we all now operate. That holds true for companies who need to develop people in order to compete; support innovation; or just generally to be more efficient and get the best out of people.

Is regular review a practicality?

I'm sure some of you reading these research findings are thinking............"that's ok for some businesses, but I can't even get my people to conduct a review conversation once per year – so how on earth will I get people to conduct regular reviews, it's just not practical."

That's a valid concern. But you need to consider why people hate those annual performance appraisals so much. It's precisely because they don't work that they avoid doing them. They're historical and out of date. Consequently they can become combative because subordinates think it's a 'do or die' moment. They certainly involve a lot of form filling and box ticking. Line managers avoid doing them because they see them as a waste of precious management time. No leader 'worth their salt' allocates precious time to non-value add activities.

However, if you could transition to a new regime, where regular short informal coaching conversations became the preferred method of managing performance............your line managers could be persuaded to allocate time when they saw real value in becoming agile; hitting those ever changing objectives and developing their people in real time. I'm prepared to bet that the average line manager could see the value in those conversations, and would carry them through regularly. Especially if they realised they would never have to do those dreaded annual appraisals ever again.

In my view, we all have to concentrate as leaders on answering the one key question................which is in the head (mostly unexpressed......but there nevertheless) of every employee all the time. That question is the subject of Chapter 4.

SUMMARY POINTS :

- Are you thinking of changing the format of your performance management framework?

- Are you still clinging to outdated principles of fixed objectives and backward looking annual review?

- Have you acknowledged that annual performance appraisal is despised and must change?

- Do you wish to be more agile in developing your people to meet the changing needs of your business and its customers?

- Could you envision your line managers giving time to brief regular developmental coaching and performance discussions?

YOUR ACTION :

- Consider what it would be like in your own organisation if you had a performance management system which actually worked!!!

4. THE QUESTION WHICH SITS IN EVERYONE'S HEAD

"HOW AM I DOING?"

"The bad news is that ignoring the performance of people is almost as bad as shredding their effort in front of their eyes...........the good news is that by simply looking at something that somebody has done, scanning it and saying 'uhuh'........you dramatically improve people's motivations." Dom Ariely

"The truth is, the once a year approach to performance isn't fun." Elias Rassi

"When feedback is included as part of regular ongoing performance discussions throughout the year, the employee, the manager, and the organisation are all better off." Shawna McKnight

"All the best assessment models, talent management tools and career plans in the world, are only as effective as the people executing them." Church & Waclawski

"Make feedback normal, not a performance review." Ed Batista

Performance Appraisal's death has been prematurely reported

I grow increasingly concerned at the simplistic headlines, in a variety of management and business articles, stating that 'Annual Performance Appraisal is dead and buried'. Such articles normally quote Microsoft; Google; Accenture and Deloitte as examples and do little in the way of explaining what replaces stopping the dreaded annual performance appraisal. As you, the reader, will now know, none of these businesses in the vanguard of change has ceased managing the performance of their people. They merely do it on a much more frequent and informal basis.

It is also fascinating to me, that whilst 98% of U.S. firms (canvassed in a poll) felt that Annual Performance Appraisal was ineffective, only a mere 6% had actually ceased conducting them!!

Leaders are often enduringly traditional! Organisations institutionalise long standing management practises, even when they provoke dissatisfaction, and are palpably unfit for purpose. I recently encountered a Construction company where the HR Team were particularly pleased with themselves for achieving 86% of annual performance appraisals completed by the year-end deadline. They had used an edict, presumably supported by the CEO, which said that no manager would be paid their year-end performance bonus unless all the annual performance appraisals had been completed for their teams. They thought that this was a real coup! My reaction was that they were enforcing the wrong system which was hated and ineffective. I also felt for the 14% of managers who were prepared to forego their own annual performance bonus for the sake of not conforming. Those managers must have felt pretty negative about appraisals not to conform!

Leaders often tell me that they are just 'too busy' to conduct the many considerable hours that Annual Appraisals take, because they see them as 'wasted time' spent on a process which just doesn't work.

What are Employees thinking about their performance?

If employees hate Annual Appraisals, what are they really thinking about performance at work? It is perfectly obvious to me what every employee is thinking. I have been an employee for many years myself, and I know what I was thinking. I have also spent many years managing teams and leading others. The question in our heads............all the time (sometimes more front of mind than others – depending on what is happening)............... is "how does my boss think that I'm doing?"

After that key pitch to a customer. After that report and piece of analysis I did. After proposing that change to our processes. After that presentation to the Board. After...........whatever it is you have just done................ you desire feedback on how it went in your bosses view. It is important to us. We don't go around asking every time, but nevertheless it is an unspoken desire.

One of the great pleasure of my life as an author and speaker; consulting in businesses and mentoring executives...............is that I get genuine feedback on how I'm doing. No one needs to play 'corporate games' with me. I realise they used to 'play me' when I was an Executive Director...............because they were playing out their career. In such circumstances, some people will feel the need to be sycophantic and tell you you're great, even if you're not. When people say to me now that my presentation was a real 'wow' – they mean it. My clients speak as they find. I'm no longer an employee so there is no need to 'sugar the pill' or to keep me sweet. I love that real feedback, because people say what they really believe.

In my work today, I regularly ask clients........... "How did I do? Did my Masterclass hit the spot for you? Did my mentoring provide helpful insights"? I require people to tell me, and they do. I ask for feedback after every piece of work, because you're only as good as the last thing you did for someone. When you don't belong to a salary payroll, you only get work if people recommend you by word of mouth....................that means people need to be saying your work was fantastic. Feedback is therefore critical.

In the world of employment, people have no less need for the answer to the question "How am I doing?" It's just that many in house processes dictate that you only get that answer once per year!!! Absurd isn't it?

<u>A perfect example of how not to give feedback</u>

I was sat in a Motorway coffee shop a couple of years ago, having broken my journey to get my morning coffee, and have a quick scan of the news in the Times.

To my expanding astonishment, into the coffee shop and onto the table next to me (in very close proximity) came a guy in a suit with a clip board, followed by an employee of the Motorway Service Station in overalls. I quickly realised, because the Manager had a Document in his clip board titled 'Annual Appraisal', that he was going to conduct this poor guy's appraisal conversation right next to me. I should really have captured this on camera with my phone, but I was too fascinated to move.

I had intended to stop for 15 minutes to drink my coffee, but I found myself fascinated by this scene of 'how not to give feedback'. The manager with the clipboard told the employee "this is your Annual Performance Appraisal". I was sat thinking, surely not here in a public place, and so close anyone could hear every single word! He then proceeded to work through a multi-page document, writing his comments and ticking boxes. The employee looked incredibly unimpressed and never uttered one word throughout the process. The employee's body language told me he definitely didn't want to be there. He was asked by his manager to sign the completed appraisal document, before sloping off back to work. He appeared totally demotivated by the whole event, certainly not invigorated or stimulated. No doubt his manager felt he had got the job done...............another box ticked. For me, the horrified observer, it was a perfect example of 'how not to' conduct an annual performance appraisal.

I wonder whether Leaders realise the power of regular feedback?

I'm by no means sure that we all understand how desperately we need to answer that unspoken question in our people's head...... "How am I doing?"

Clearly my Motorway Service station example showed an employee who wasn't getting regular feedback. His Annual Performance Appraisal was conducted in the wrong place, and in a very dictatorial style. Such poor quality feedback was blatently a complete waste of time, yet I suspect it might be typical of so many interactions between boss and subordinates.

Yet, we must not forget that employees do want to know how they are doing. Regular feedback can be the life-blood of healthy coaching conversations, and the development of the potential of your people. It can also be a key to better performance in the fast moving modern world in which we all operate. Regular feedback is a means of gaining incremental improvements in performance, as each piece of work is undertaken and completed. Dialogue between the leader and the led should be regular, informal, and part of the natural rhythm of the workplace.

SUMMARY POINTS :

- Don't read into the headlines that big names have stopped performance management in their businesses

- Many organisations want to jettison Annual Performance Appraisal – but don't know what to replace it with

- Employees regularly want to know how you rate the work they are doing. It matters to them, even if they don't say that to you. It's the unspoken question.

- Bureaucratic, once per year 'form filling' appraisals fulfil little or no real purpose – and are despised by the doers and the done to!

YOUR ACTIONS :

- Do you, as a Leader, realise the importance of feedback, regularly given, relevant to the work? It develops your people and delivers better performance.

- Will you commit to a change of process?

5. FEEDBACK IS BOTH NECESSARY AND WANTED

FEEDBACK BECOMES FEED FORWARD

"Feedback is the breakfast of Champions." Ken Blanchard

"We all need people who will give us feedback...... that's how we improve." Bill Gates

"Make feedback normal, not a performance review." Ed Batista

"To be effective and yield results for your business, performance management must be a continuous year-round process with no end." Teala Wilson

"Companies need to shift their approach by creating a culture, where regular performance feedback discussions are the norm." Melany Gallant

"If you are building a culture where honest expectations are communicated & peer accountability is the norm, then the group will address poor performance & attitudes." Henry Cloud

The Power of Regular Feedback

This Chapter begins with some powerful quotes. I'm fully with Bill Gates on this............we all need feedback in order to be able to improve.

I also fully believe that those performance management conversations need to be part of the normal routine way of life in an organisation. Performance cannot possibly be effectively managed, arising from a once per year conversation. That concept is, and always has been ludicrous!

I'm reminded of speaking at a conference on the topic of 'Giving Feedback'. I spoke alongside an Olympic High board diver, his role being to speak on feedback in sport, mine to speak on feedback in business. Never appear alongside an Olympian, because everyone in the audience just wants a 'selfie' with the Olympian – alongside the Olympic medal of course. Despite that minor irritation, he was a thoroughly nice regular guy, and had some interesting things to say about feedback in the world of sport.

He explained to the audience that, as a diver, he needed feedback from his coach after every dive that he made. How did he enter the water; how was his body positioned; and a variety of other factors. That feedback was certainly both wanted, and needed, if he was to improve his diving performance. For him, feedback was very necessary to feed-forward.

For an Olympian, it is obvious that regular feedback and coaching feeds into higher performance. Is that not also true of jobs in the workplace? Of course it is!!

C.I.P.D. Research Report 'Could do better': What works in Performance Management

The Chartered Institute of Personnel & Development, my own Institute, has conducted some research into performance evaluation. They too have been commenting about some big well-known companies abandoning their Annual Appraisal processes, and replacing them with more frequent informal discussions.

The review of the academic research into this topic has been conducted by Jonny Gifford of the C.I.P.D. This involved a meta-analysis of dozens of academic studies into the topic, in order to remove the 'hype' from the reality of what works in performance management.

This new study suggests that feedback does make a net positive contribution to performance at work. Jonny Gifford states, however, that there is a huge variance between different types of feedback, and that much of the literature on the topic is misunderstood.

Gifford asserts that some of the loathing around the performance appraisal process is because of the way it is carried out. He states that "it is crucial that managers feed back to their people on how they are progressing toward their goals". The many calls to axe annual appraisals are only part of the story.

Gifford's report also concurs with my own strongly held view, that regular, less formal conversations are particularly effective. He says that "performance management should be seen as a continuous chain of connected activities, not as a discreet process that is only occasionally visited."

Another point on which I agree with Gifford, from personal experience, is that employee self-assessed performance is best avoided, since it is inherently biased. I always found that individuals over estimate how well they were doing, and some of the conversation was spent talking them down from a higher position. That is never motivational. Gifford found, from his research, that updating individuals on their progress could be effective via digital dashboards; goal Apps or face to face conversations..................as long as these took place as part of an overall holistic ongoing and regular process.

C.I.P.D. Research Report 'Could do better' : Goal Setting and Feedback

One of Jonny Gifford's major research findings in 'Could do better', is around the important topic of goal setting.

Those vanguard Companies in the Tech. world, who have moved to regular performance management, have found that goals can hinder innovation and agile working.

Gifford's research suggests that goal setting can be extremely powerful (we all know about setting SMART goals), but they can detract from what needs to be done in complex tasks (much like the Tech. Company world). In a fast moving complex environment, Gifford's research found that "do your best" directives and goals focussed on learning, do more to help employees perform well.

Leaders have to think about the nature of work. Clear, specific objectives related to the big picture can be powerful and energising, if that fits the nature of the work in the organisation. However, if all that matters is agility/ innovation and speed (the ability to get ahead of the competition) in a highly complex environment............. then specific objectives might hold your best people back. The Leader has to judge the nature of the work first and foremost. In highly volatile and complex environments, a strategy of hiring individuals who are quick to learn/develop, and cope with setbacks.................... plus releasing them to do their best, is a vital coping strategy.

What you and I might have originally thought was obvious, about goal setting and feedback, certainly deserves further consideration.

In many sectors, the nature of work is fast changing – and so must our long held beliefs about our work processes – especially managing performance.

Getting feedback right to improve performance

One of the conclusions in Gifford's meta-analysis of the research was that, in many cases, feedback had no effect or worsens performance!

We have already discussed that getting performance feedback right is crucially important. Also, we acknowledged that individuals desire feedback on how they are doing. It is also important to take employee feedback about the fairness/effectiveness and usefulness of the discussion process. Managing performance is a two way street.

Moreover, it is vitally important to train line managers in techniques for conducting effective coaching and performance discussions. People do not necessarily say or do the right thing 'intuitively'. All leaders benefit from hints and tips for conducting great conversations to get a good performance outcome.

I personally favour a strengths based approach for giving feedback – and Gifford's research supports this concept. I particularly like the strengths based framework developed by Marcus Buckingham – who has a very effective tool called 'strengths finder' on the market.

My own mantra about effective regular feedback, is to always leave the individual with their self-respect intact, at the end of any conversation on performance. Your people need regular coaching tips from you concerning 'how to' improve, and regular check-in time to talk about 'how it's going'. Employees need to feel the performance conversations are motivating.............and listening to what they say will reveal to the perceptive line manager how effective the performance conversation has been. Managers need training on how to conduct these effective conversations about performance. As I said previously, Leaders are not born with the necessary skills to do this well.

Getting feedback wrong and sending performance backward

If you took some time to read the research work of Denisi and Kluger, they give Leaders food for thought on giving feedback. Their finding suggested that feedback often either achieved nothing, or worse still made things worse more often than feedback actually improved performance.

The research of Denisi and Kluger dates back to the 1990's, and presents a rather negative perspective on feedback. However, I think it does serve to give a very clear insight on what goes wrong with feedback in the workplace in so many instances. In the real world, I believe that very few line managers focus on strengths, and nor do they emphasise what they would like to see more of in behavioural terms.

My own finding and observation is that leaders tend to be hard wired to focus on what is wrong, and what isn't working. Simply pointing this out to the exclusion of all else doesn't necessarily change the behaviour of those getting that feedback. The natural instinct of the employee will be to defend against the threat of bad feedback, and retort with deflection strategies. They may even choose to not hear it at all. People don't necessarily change behaviour just because they are told to. They are more likely to change and improve when they are encouraged to see insights into what benefits change will bring about. They will also respond better in an environment of mutual understanding.

Developing a mindset for effective 21st Century feedback

To my mind, leaders need to be developing a whole new mindset concerning performance management and feedback appropriate for today's complex organisational environments.

Continuing the worst of the 20th Century view of some leaders........ that 'beating people will continue until performance improves'...................harks back to the galley slave masters of yesteryear. This view of performance has long since been outmoded, and no elements of this will 'hack it' into the 21st Century!

I want to ask whether you are developing a new way of giving feedback in your own organisation? Is it fit for purpose? Does it work across age ranges? Does it work at present?

There are considerable performance gains to be had from changing the way feedback is conducted by line managers. The more they learn to do this well, and to do it on a regular 'business as usual' basis................... the more leaders will see productivity gains.

I trust I have illustrated for you, from the research findings, that there are significant negative performance dips to be encountered, by continuing to use feedback as a 'stick' with which to beat people. Effective organisations in the 21st Century, will be those who train their leaders to conduct effective coaching conversations, which stimulate and encourage higher performance.

Are you one of those leaders, who has recognised the new 'rules of the performance management game'? Or are you still enforcing an outdated 'box ticking' appraisal system which you know doesn't really work at all?

SUMMARY POINTS :

- Do you realise the vital importance of regular positive coaching, and feedback to drive performance?

- Did you know that all the academic research studies point to the importance of regular ongoing performance management?

- Are you still setting goals in the same way you have always done...........or do you give learning and development goals for complex/fast changing work?

- Do you use a 'strength finder' type tool in your organisation to coach individuals?

- Are your feedback sessions making matters worse or better?

- Are your leaders trained to conduct effective performance coaching conversations?

YOUR ACTIONS :

- Consider getting training yourself on how to give effective feedback.....................and cascade that to all your leaders

- Institute a discipline of regular coaching conversations in the organisation.................using appropriate tools and objectives

6. FACING CONFLICT IN MANAGING PERFORMANCE

SOMETIMES THERE ARE BIG PROBLEMS TO BE TACKLED WITH AN INDIVIDUAL UNDERPERFORMER

"Peace is not the absence of conflict, it is the ability to handle conflict by peaceful means." Ronald Reagan

"The better able team members are to engage, speak, listen, hear, interpret, and respond constructively – the more likely their teams are to leverage conflict, than be levelled by it." Runde & Flanagan

"No pressure, no diamonds." Mary Case

"The more we run from conflict, the more it masters us; the more we try to avoid it, the more it controls us; the less we fear conflict, the less it confuses us; the less we deny our differences, the less they divide us." David Augsburger

"Difficulties are meant to rouse, not discourage. The human spirit is to grow stronger by conflict." William Ellery Channing

<u>Leaders need to exercise 'Tough Love'</u>

If our 'executive radar' tells us there is a major underperformance problem with an individual in the organisation ....our role as Leaders is to face into that issue, rather than the usual default of ignoring it, or working around it. There will certainly be massive expectations from our workforce that we will deal with it.

Although I have argued so far, that we should positively play to strengths in our feedback – sometimes we will all be faced with a major performance issue of this type with a key person. The issue will be obvious, and the issue will be serious. If you 'duck it', then your currency as a Leader will fall, and the performance of your whole workforce will suffer. You may never hear it said, but conversations over coffee will mutter "why should we bother........X gets away with murder".

Based upon the conversations I have had with numerous CEOs over the past 10 years, I strongly believe that facing into conflict and serious underperformance in people is something which all Leaders find very difficult. I have never yet met a CEO who said that they took action too soon! They all tell me that they waited far too long, and openly say that they were too cautious. I spoke in Chapter 1 about all the reasons for not facing into underperformance, and in this Chapter, I want to tackle the issue head on.

My recommendation to Leaders fearful of conflict, is that they need to exhibit 'tough love'. The tough part is pretty obvious. Leaders need to force themselves to overcome their fear, and face into the issue. The 'love' part, means that you don't have to become aggressive or downright nasty to effectively deal with conflict. That is a stereotype which is not helpful.

Indeed, the more you can remain factual, logical and unemotional during difficult conversations – the better you will become at conducting those conversations. During tough conversations, the individual on the receiving end will frequently become defensive and emotional. As Leader of the conversation, this means preparing your facts well beforehand, and calmly putting your finger on the problem with corroborative evidence.

Good preparation is essential for any meeting, negotiation or presentation that you make. Facing into conflict and underperformance is exactly the same. Do your homework. Take advice from experts. Anticipate the potential range of responses, defences and pitfalls. Prepare how you will respond in each scenario. If you conduct this level of preparation, it will boost your confidence in facing into the problem.

Also, don't forget to come out of any such conflict conversation with mutual respect intact. That's the 'tough love' part – and it is possible if you do it well.

During my 35 years in corporate life, I was involved in many dismissal situations personally. Sometimes the initial dismissal was mine to conduct, sometimes I was adjudicating dismissal appeals from the ex-employee. My aim, at the outset of any such circumstance, was to emerge with an ongoing relationship with the individual.

Even when parting company with employees, I was keen to help those individuals to move on, and get into a new role where they might better succeed.

Clearly, it is not always possible for a good outcome. If the individual reacts badly, and is determined to blame the organisation for their situation, then it is rarely going to end well. Some individuals are determined to be aggressive and fight the business. That is for sure. However, I found that there were always individuals who departed professionally, accepted ongoing help, and maintained an ongoing relationship after the trauma of losing their job with the organisation. 'Tough love' can have a very positive outcome if you aim for that result. There are those who realise that the role and the organisation was not for them, and that they are much happier working somewhere else. Those type of people are likely to return and thank you for relieving them of considerable strain, and helping them into a better suited situation.

'Tough love' needs to be the strategy of the Leader in facing serious underperformers. At least the process will begin in the right way. The outcome is then determined by the reaction of the subordinate.

The story of the reluctant Policeman

I had opportunity a few years ago, to work with the Leadership of a Police Force in the U.K. I was running a series of programmes as part of a Masterclass on Culture and Performance, which took place over a period of about 9 months.

In one particular session, I was talking to an audience of the top 90 Police Officers, discussing how to deal with serious underperformers, whilst also pushing talent. The heart of the topic of performance management.

I was stopped from speaking by an intervention from one of the senior Police Officers in the audience. He felt the need to point out that my 'private sector' perspective on performance management wasn't relevant to his situation in the 'public sector' Police Force. He said that he felt that my experience in Asda, for instance, was all about a fast moving retail business, in the private sector, where facing into performance was the norm.

"You come from an environment where 'hire and fire' is the way things work. I work in the public sector, where it is almost impossible to get fired for underperformance, and underperforming individuals are tolerated. I have a couple of underperforming individuals in my team (Whom I inherited) and I know they have been underperformers for years. I don't think what you are saying to us about dealing with underperformers is that easy in the Police Force."

It was a passionate speech, and the rest of the audience were pretty much acquiescent. I could tell that they agreed with him. This was one of those 'moments' where it was time to make a response that would be both helpful – but also to point out his error of judgement. I let a few seconds elapse whilst gathering my thoughts, and then I told him that I thought he was wrong. I said that I believed that Leaders often constrain themselves by believing they were less powerful than in reality they were. I told him that I believed in 'tough love', and that I believed in facing into conflict situations in the right way (of which the conversation with him in front of 90 of his peers was just one such!!).

I advised him that part of the problem lay with his own mindset, believing he was impotent to change the 'system', and accepting the mantra that no one ever tackles underperformance in the Police Force. I asked him to think about deciding to take action and not accept that normative mindset. I said that I wanted him to go away and take advice from relevant Legal/HR experts in the Police as to how to tackle the underperformance problem individuals in his team. I urged him to get 'stuck into the problem' using 'tough love'.

There was quite a bit of muttering by others in the audience, and I could tell that not everyone accepted that it was that simple. Nevertheless, we moved the session forward to discuss other areas of the Masterclass, and the 'moment' passed.

I had forgotten all about my challenge to the Policeman and his underperforming team members, when I went back to the same 90 senior Police team members 3 months later. I was there to deliver a different Masterclass on a topic which had nothing to do with performance management. Right on the front row was sat my senior Policeman – and I suddenly remembered our conversation 3 months earlier. After I was introduced, up went this guy's hand, and he asked to say a few words to everyone gathered in the audience. In those few seconds, I wondered if this would be a good or bad start to the session!! Anyway, I said to him "Please do".

The senior Policeman proceeded to remind everyone what he had challenged me about 3 months earlier. He reminded them about how he had said that it was much more difficult to deal with serious underperformance in the Police, than in the private sector. He then surprised me by telling the audience, of his peers, that he had been completely wrong in his view! He had felt challenged by my assertion that it was his own beliefs about what he could or could not do that was holding him back. He had realised that he was allowing 'the system' to render him impotent to act. He told the audience how he had taken professional advice; gotten himself thoroughly prepared...............and then faced into the conflict of tackling those 2 long term underperformance problem individuals. He told us that one of those people was no longer with the Police Force, and that the other had been a turnaround in performance which was nothing short of miraculous.

There was a murmur of approval for his actions from the audience (and an internal sigh of relief for me) which I turned into a round of applause for this coura-geous man. This was clearly a success story, despite belief originally that 'you can't buck the system'.

However, as the applause died down, our senior Policeman remained standing..............he hadn't finished his story. He wanted to endorse and emphasise my point; that this action had not only faced into the 2 issues; but he wanted to talk about the effect upon the rest of his team. The effect of his actions and the resulting performance of his team had been 'electrified'. The team, apparently, were buzzing. He had been given numerous comments about being the first Leader they had worked for who had faced into those 2, and he was regarded as something of a 'local hero' by the team, for what he had done. Because of what he had done, the morale of the whole team had been lifted, and people were saying "at last – someone has faced into the problem."

This intervention beautifully started my Masterclass with those senior Police, but more importantly, made the point that every Leader (regardless of public or private sector or context) can take action on serious underperformance......they merely have to choose to do so.

Natural Conflict Avoidance affects business performance

Avoiding or procrastinating on serious performance issues affects many more employees than just the individual concerned. The workforce (your workforce is always watching Leader behaviour – more than you could ever imagine) expect timely action, and if you take that action, it will inevitably lift the performance of everyone.

Some Leaders tend to believe that only the CEO and the Board know about senior performance issues. This is a complete fallacy. Everyone in the organisation is aware of everyone else, and serious underperformance issues are widely realised. Employees expect Leaders to take action in such circumstances, and inaction causes everyone to perform less well than they might otherwise. Performance is to a degree 'discounted' by lack of leadership action.

The fear of conflict is very real in the minds of many Leaders. Coupled with the fact that facing into issues is very time consuming; has risks and unknowns ....and that many Leaders don't really have the necessary skills to do this well.................means it is all too easy for the Leaders to let other priorities intervene. The underperformance issue goes into the 'too difficult' pile, for handling later.

However, I want to remind you, that avoidance is a serious Leadership error. Do not underestimate how much this can be a drag on the performance of the watching organisation.

People will not respect you if you leave a serious underperformance problem un-tackled. Conversely, do not underestimate the opposite effect. Taking advice; marshalling your facts; preparing reaction scenarios and using 'tough love' to tackle the issue...................will make you a hero in the eyes of your people............and performance will lift as a consequence.

This is one of those matters facing Executives, which is so often mishandled. Your personal reputation will suffer if this is the case for you, and overall performance will degrade. However, if you step up, and give time and the effort required to face into serious issues – your standing will increase, and the performance of the business will benefit overall. Why not determine to be that rarity? A CEO or Leader who is brave enough to do this well, and reap the rewards. Be the first Leader to tell me – "yes, I acted early, and wow has that made a difference."

SUMMARY POINTS :

- Do you exhibit 'tough love' when faced with serious performance issues?

- Aim to face into issues by getting good advice and making good preparations

- Set out with the aim of having a positive relationship with the individual – even if you have to part company

- Don't underestimate the drain on your credibility and the negative effect upon overall performance in procrastinating on serious performance issues

- Don't underestimate the positivity for you as a leader, and for overall performance when you take action on serious performance problems

- Remember – everyone knows the serious problems, and everyone is watching – all the time. This is never invisible.

YOUR ACTIONS :

- Do you realise how important facing into underperformance is in your own organisation?

- Determine personally to make a step change in your own Leadership courage

7. TALENT MANAGEMENT IS ALL ABOUT 'PUSHING YOUR TALENT' TO ACHIEVE THEIR POTENTIAL

TALENT MANAGEMENT IS A SUBSET OF PERFORMANCE MANGEMENT

"Developing Talent is the most important task of a business – the 'sine qua non' of competition in a knowledge economy." Peter Drucker

"Talent Management needs as much focus as Capital Management in corporations." Jack Welch

"There is no way to spend too much time on obtaining and developing the best people." Larry Bossidy

"Talent Management is more than just a competitive advantage; it is a fundamental requirement for business to succeed." Silzer & Dowell

"Of course companies need to determine who the future leaders & high potentials are, but to accomplish this at the expense of alienating others, hurts the entire organisation." Josh Bersin

"People are not your most important asset – the right people are." Jim Collins

Don't forget your Talent – Spot it and Develop it

Much of performance management focuses on underperformance, when at least half of it should focus on over performance, and those who are outperforming, or have the potential to outperform.

I have already written about the need to be balanced with your feedback, and to play to individual strengths. I've also referred to the need to face into serious underperformers – particularly because of the way they affect the morale and effort of the whole workforce around them.

However, Leaders should never lose sight of the talent in the business, and the need to manage those people for optimum performance. Leaders should always give time to identifying talent, and then seeking to maximise the impact of those individuals.

I think it's a great maxim to ask people in your organisation to be 'self-developers', and make them responsible for devising their own personal development plan. I don't believe that the organisation should be all knowing/paternalistic and the provider of all your development. There is so much knowledge and information available on line for the potential learner. Those who are self-motivated can learn a great deal in their own time which used to be delivered by training course attendance. If people invest in themselves, I am always more inclined to weigh in and help. If they expect the business to spoon feed them, then the converse applies.

It is even more important to challenge Leaders with spotting and developing talent. If you are a self-developer, and are challenged with spotting/developing others, you are generally more likely to take up the cause. Any performance appraisal discussion 'worth its salt', will challenge a leader to articulate whom they have identified with potential, and what they are doing to develop them.

<u>Does your Performance Appraisal discussion process challenge Leaders to develop others?</u>

When I worked for Asda, we challenged our Store Managers to identify 6 individuals from the shop floor level each year, who they viewed as having talent for leadership. They were asked to begin nurturing them, by giving them exposure to mini projects, and letting them take charge of organising small pieces of work. This was not about being promoted, nor about being given more money, it was a mechanism which exposed people to opportunity to prove they had something in them.

It's amazing what you find out about the potential of an individual, when you expose them to opportunity. This is not about making a decision about promoting people, it's about giving them chances to show what they can do in day to day business life. Project work happens in all business contexts, but using projects as a Talent development tool is a way of thinking about project work differently. Often, we use the usual suspects, or always the best people, rather than adding some new names into the mix.

I wonder whether you challenge your L
developing talent in this informal and dy
Do you use project work as a way of testin
talent?

Talent Programmes – frequently the 'kiss of death'

I have seen so many examples of Talent identification
which both ruin talented people, and at the same time,
switch off great swathes of other people in the
organisation who become 'non talent' by default.

Leaders have looked at me with incredulity, when
I advised them not to have a formal 'High Potential
Talent Programme'. I agree with Josh Bersin's quote at
the head of this Chapter…….. "of course companies
need to determine who the future leaders and high
potentials are, but to accomplish this at the expense of
alienating others, hurts the entire organisation."

I have first-hand experience of seeing the identified
'Talent' gaining a sense of having 'arrived'…………..
becoming arrogant………..and their effort/drive for
success reducing accordingly. Worse still, their personal
leadership style corrodes, because they begin to 'Lord it'
over other lesser mortals who are deemed to be less
capable. At the same time, the whole exercise, if we're not
very careful, has the enormous potential to label everyone
else in the organisation as 'not talented'. This can be mas-
sively demotivational, and counter-productive. This is a
real 'lose-lose-lose' situation…………….and is obviously
one to be avoided. Hence my advice to Leaders to
beware!!!

The 'Talent' in an organisation, is actually everyone you employ. Top class Leaders realise this, and the fact that they need to get the best from everyone on the payroll. Don't fall into the classic trap of creating a few 'prima-donnas', but do seek to get the best from all your people. Give small project opportunities and tasks with visibility and exposure to Leadership to those whom you believe might have potential for the future. Challenge your Leaders to spot and identify people in their own teams who might have potential – and discuss these individuals in your management meetings. My advice, based upon years of experience, is not to burden your organisation with some expensive high profile 'Talent Programme' for the few (with all the pitfalls just discussed), but to have a strategy which is much more low key (and much more effective) at identifying and developing talent.

Talent Development at a practical level

One of my 'pet hates' when I go into various companies occurs when I see their company values on a wall plaque. To be fair, a few that I observe are simple and effective, and more importantly.......the people inside the organisation know those values and live them. Unfortunately, so many of the ones I see are complex, lengthy 'management gobbledegook'. Sadly, they are not known by the workforce, are impossible to remember and incredibly longwinded. Consequently, they cannot be acted upon by employees in such circumstances........and are therefore pointless. This phenomenon is at its worst (and I have experienced this all too often) when even the Directors and Leaders in the organisation can't remember them all. What chance does the rest of the organisation have?

Chief amongst this 'pet hate' of ineffective Values statements, is the classic phrase used about people working in the organisation. All of you who are reading this book will know this phrase which I loathe (maybe some of you are even using it!!)................because I come across it with such regularity. This is that politically correct slogan "our people are our greatest asset." The reason I loathe the phrase is not its ubiquity, it's the fact that no one really means it. I know this because companies always list it last of their list of company value statements! By definition, if you really value something, you would not put it last in the list. People cannot and should not be an afterthought........if you really value Talent development, then think about this and how it relates to your own Company Values.

Such Value statements are classic errors in the management of talent, and employees can see through them. These are errors great Leaders shouldn't make. I would urge anyone in a Leadership position to avoid platitudes and jargon, especially when it comes to talking about people. Authentic language, which you are able and prepared to live out on a daily basis, is what your people need.

Talent development needs to be practical and easily implemented. I have seen a number of organisations successfully implement a regular review of both performance and potential; discussed at Board level, and actioned through Board directors. Talent development must be through the line, and not something held within a H.R. function. Leaders need to identify those with potential in their teams, and be managing their careers accordingly, through everyday projects and business.

Spotting Talent and Managing Careers

All too often, internal promotions and new appointments into organisations are far too hasty. Vacancies in key roles drive a sort of organisational frenzy to get the job filled. Executives feel compelled to fill a gap, rather than making sure that vacancy is only filled by really 'top notch' talent which fits the culture of the organisation.

I believe that those organisations that have regular/ structured talent and potential discussions, are far more proactive in filling vacancies from the talent within the business, and developing the careers of individuals across the organisational silos (which are so prone to rule out the sharing of internal talent lest the silo be depleted). I'm not suggesting you should never hire new talent into your organisation. Often, an infusion of new skills/abilities, or a catalyst for change is absolutely the right thing to do. However, external hiring should not be the 1st and only reflex of the organisation to a vacancy occurring. External hiring is a high risk situation, both in terms of organisational fit, and the capabilities of the individual being hired. Hiring is both subjective and difficult with any external candidate, and all Executives are prone to mistakes when hiring.

I would propose, to any organisation examining internal versus external candidates, that there should be a target ratio of say 70/30 or 60/40 or 80/20........depending upon the strength and depth of your own internal talent pool. It is a powerful statement to say to your internal people that the majority of vacancies will be filled from internal talent/rising stars, with the remainder coming from external hires. It is a great motivator to those of your people who want to pursue their careers within the organisation, to know that the company will look extensively to fill roles from within..........before flying to the headhunters, or various other methods of external hiring.

Talent Management – mean it – nurture it

Leaders have to be serious about managing talent. It is no use having platitudes on a plaque on the wall of your entrance foyer! People in the organisation need to know that you mean what you say, and more importantly, that you will do what you say you will do.

Careers matter to people, and in an age of increasing disloyalty and job hopping.........one sure way to better retain talent, is for people to know that you really do have their career interests at heart. If you are seen to spend time spotting talent and making good career moves happen for good people, it sends all the right messages to the whole organisation. When good people are promoted early and given opportunities they deserve, then it lifts the performance of everyone in the organisation. In my experience, people never resent the good individuals 'getting on'. They all feel that they are working in a meritocracy, and that their workplace is a 'development cauldron'. People begin to see that if they prove themselves, through project work and other assignments, they will get their opportunity also. This type of working environment builds a high performance workplace.

This is something of a leadership philosophy. I meet many Executives who merely look to fill roles with the talent on the open market. I also meet a lot of Executives who complain that there isn't enough of the right talent on the market!! I wonder....................are you one of those Executives? Far fewer of the Executives I encounter, are the type who can articulate plans to develop the career path of their existing people.......... seeking future talent from within. It is even rarer to find Executives and CEOs who are aiming for a particular ratio (say 70/30) of internal to external talent. Many tell me they haven't got the talent within........but is this the chicken or the egg? That for me is the essence of the outworking of real practical Talent management.

Marcus Buckingham at Deloitte

One of my favourite authors and management thinkers is Marcus Buckingham, as mentioned previously. As I said, I like his 'strength-finder' tool. People who play to their particular strengths are a source of competitive advantage; higher performance and to accessing their discretionary effort. Those people able to do what they love best, tend never to feel as if they are working a day in their lives.

Marcus Buckingham's work is research based. That is principally why I like it. Marcus has done extensive work at Deloitte (who themselves are at the vanguard of developing regular informal performance appraisal conversations), aided by his self-assessment strengths finder tool. Deloitte were previously spending 2 million hours per year, as an organisation, on performance appraisals (in the old once per year formal style), and were extremely dissatisfied with the results.

Regular conversations, with an emphasis on talent development, have produced a systematic, yet informal approach that the Leadership at Deloitte feel is far more productive. Also, Deloitte employees feel the process is much more useful and motivational. That is not a response normally associated with performance management!

<u>Don't lose your best Talent because of a clunky outdated Performance Appraisal process</u>

High performers love to talk about their performance. For this group of employees, it is an opportunity for recognition by their line manager. The worst thing for your best Talent, is an archaic system which only provides space for this once per annum! They will tend to feel underestimated, and that their outperformance has been disregarded. This helps to make them feel they want to take their talents elsewhere.

Much of the data analysis I have seen, shows that some 60% of existing performance management systems fail to correctly identify high performers, and suitably motivate them. Surely, it is a tragic consequence, if your own internal performance management system is the very thing which causes your best talent to become disillusioned and defect to the competition.

I firmly believe that Executives need a 'wake up' call, in order to get on board with the seismic changes which are taking place with Performance Appraisal processes. Those organisations in the vanguard of this change will retain and attract the best Talent, and thereby their competitive edge.

Are you still running a clunky once per annum Performance Appraisal process? Does it fail to identify Talent, and switch off your very best people? If your answer to any of these questions is yes.........then it is time to change tack.

SUMMARY POINTS :

- Do you challenge your Leaders to spot in-house Talent and develop it?

- Do you give in-house Talent exposure to projects and leading project teams?

- Have you got a Talent programme which costs you, yet switches off many others in your business?

- Don't harbour those nonsense Value statements 'our people are our most important asset' – set out how you will develop Talent in a practical way

- Spot Talent at all levels – be known for helping to develop the careers of the best in your business

- Decide on an internal versus external job-filling ratio and manage it accordingly – tell your people!

- Realise that clunky Annual Performance appraisal is one factor in losing some of your best Talent

YOUR ACTIONS :

- Determine to be a Talent developer

- Make it a requirement of your Leaders around you also – challenge them to spot and develop Talent

8. THE EMERGING CONCENSUS

FREQUENT INFORMAL REVIEWS DURING ONE TO ONE DISCUSSIONS WITH THE LINE MANAGER ARE THE WAY FORWARD FOR THE 21st CENTURY

"Managers don't like giving appraisals, and employees don't like receiving them. Perhaps they're not liked because both parties suspect what the evidence has proved for decades. Traditional annual performance appraisals don't work." Jeffrey Pfeffer

"Leaders need to understand that there is no good way to do annual performance appraisals. It is inherently the wrong thing to do. Leaders need to know what is wrong with performance appraisal, and what to do instead." Peter Scholtes

"Good execution of performance appraisal is not the solution. More people are realising that improving how performance appraisals are done, is an attempt to do the wrong thing better. If you insist on doing the wrong thing, I suppose you might as well do it better – but how about not doing the wrong thing at all?" John Hunter

"To be effective and yield results for your business – performance management must be an all year round process with no end." Teala Wilson

How can busy Leaders find the time?

When I say that frequent informal reviews, (during one to one conversations) are the emerging consensus...............some of you reading this will be thinking "I find it hard to set aside time for the Annual Performance Appraisals for my direct reports.......how on earth can this be practical for a busy Executive?" You probably think that committing to regular performance reviews is neither realistic, nor practical.

I know that I am, by my very nature, both realistic and practical. I would never recommend something theoretical, nor something which just wasn't practical and achievable. I believe fundamentally, that what I am about to recommend will actually take very little of your time, and the results will be more than worth the inputs. More of this shortly.

The real reason that you cannot find the time for Annual Performance Reviews : is because they are a waste of time

Annual Performance Appraisals instil a feeling of dread in most Leaders, and their direct reports. These gargantuan processes don't work, and much Academic research has backed up what many Leaders have felt for years about the process. It is a waste of Management time and effort.

A combined study by the Chartered Institute of Personnel and Development and Halogen Software, in 2015, found that only 44% of employees were set clear objectives, and 18% received no feedback whatsoever.

It is a salutary fact that most Executives and employees alike, dread the approach of 'that time of year' for the Annual Performance Appraisals to take place. Employees tend to feel that data collection and adjustments to performance should happen dynamically on the job during the year................not all in one solitary occasion covering a whole year.

Executives, in my experience, naturally gravitate toward carrying out tasks which they know will improve their business. They don't have to be forced to 'do the right things'. Because they feel that Annual Performance Appraisal sessions don't add much real value, yet steal huge chunks of their time........they tend to find excuses and avoid allocating precious time to them.

So..........how to replace this defective unsatisfactory process with a much better one.

<u>Using Business as Usual : your regular one to one discussions with your direct reports</u>

Most top class Executives have one to one discussions with their direct reports on a regular basis. The best Executives usually do this at least monthly – some even more frequently than that.

The classic one to one discussion on 'business as usual' matters is informal, dynamic and involves talking about the work issues/progress chasing/KPIs/problems with team members/solutions and so on. This is very much a check in on 'how things are going' and what may need adjustment or change. One to ones are opportunities for the free flow exchange between Leader and subordinate about all the normal 'work stuff' going on. Sometimes, when all is tracking pretty well, this will simply be a quick check in. On other occasions, when there are emerging issues, it's a chance to brainstorm solutions, bounce ideas and actions off each other, and sometimes to discuss how to tackle a major problem.

In my former corporate life, I regarded one to ones for my direct reports as a sacrosanct piece of my available time. I told my reports that I would never take that time out of my diary.......period. They could cancel if they wished, but that time with me was there for them. My last corporate job was in a business turning over £20bn, with 175,000 people in over 400 locations and I travelled around 30,000 business miles per annum.....................
with a pretty heavy set of Executive meeting diary com-mitments (Board Meetings/Strategy sessions and the like). I would challenge the reader that if I could guarantee my direct reports a monthly one to one discussion (and there is nothing special or superhuman about me) then so could you. Why not adopt my mantra, 'never cancel a one to one session.' Realise how demoralising it is to your direct reports, who will feel worthless.

Indeed, if you're not already holding regular one to ones with you direct reports, then you are missing a key tech-nique to get better performance in your own organisa-tion. I found that one to ones were a great way to build trust and rapport – to hear people talk about what they were thinking – and to agree what necessary interven-tions should be taking place over the coming month. In other words, this was management time very well spent. Indeed, I can't conceive of a better way of tracking work progress in fast moving complex environments without this type of work arrangement.

If you are already holding regular one to ones with your reports (and the best Leaders will be for sure), then it is really easy to incorporate dynamic regular performance appraisal into them. This is really about spending the last 5/10 minutes of the one to one, answering that question "how am I doing?" for your direct reports. In effect, this end of the one to one conversation becomes a mini performance appraisal. The difference is, the data and facts about the work will be bang up to date....... because you have just talked about them. By definition, this 'job/work stuff' cannot be out of date. Also, because the occasion is not a once per year 'defend or die' type of event, it takes all the tension from the discussion. In the same way that the one to one is an informal discussion about work – so the performance appraisal part of it will be as well. You are merely getting feedback from your boss about how he/she thinks you're doing. The boss is merely giving up to date feedback....it's no big deal.

The Annual Performance appraisals were always conflictual, because they were either explicitly or implicitly tied up with remuneration. Those on the receiving end were bound to argue, because this would determine pay for a year.

If the conversations are part of business as usual, feedback being given is purely on the month, and the individual can correct underperformance incrementally, or feel good about over-performance and build upon it. The facts are undeniable, the relevance is current, and the picture is built up over a sensible time period. Moreover, if performance is great – recognition can be given there and then as appropriate.

This type of dynamic regular performance coaching is happening in the vanguard companies, and they are using it to great effect. It is no coincidence that their performance is benefitting from having changed from such annoying; time consuming and fundamentally flawed Annual Performance Appraisal processes. They realise that they have saved many precious hours of management time, and also have a much more dynamic and workable system.

<u>Cumulating assessments made during one to ones :</u>
<u>saves Leadership time</u>

Giving 12 mini views of "how am I doing?" to your direct reports at the end of your one to ones, builds up a picture over 12 months.

I recommend to many of my clients, keeping a record (on a one pager) of these 'mini-assessments'. I don't mind whether you give a score each month, or write down a sentence or phrase which has 'graduated' meaning. I must admit to preferring scores personally, but I realise that some prefer to use words. Either way, your direct reports should have something on screen, or on a working document to take away from the discussion – which has taken a minute to record. Your direct reports can easily see how they are tracking. If they're ahead of average, they know what they have to do in the month to stay ahead. If they are behind, they know what they have to achieve to catch up.

This is a much more realistic, dynamic and regular performance appraisal – which is building a picture as you go. It is based on current reality, and delivered in an informal style. It is performance coaching in action. It also allows for in-year changes to the objectives set for your direct reports, as circumstances change in the business. Objectives used to be much more stable years ago.......but in today's fast moving and dynamic business environment, it is much more common for objectives to change in year. The old Annual Performance Appraisal process couldn't cope with that level of dynamism, resulting in arguments about what had changed at the beginning of the Appraisal. Using one to ones allows for discussion and flexing of objectives as circumstances change.

The saving in time for the Leader comes at the end of the business year. By simple mathematical accumulation of the one to one scoring record, there is in effect no need to sit down for that old-style conflict ridden Annual Performance Appraisal session at all! The record of the monthly one to ones can flow directly for remuneration purposes. It is even possible to cover your discussions about personal development and the development of others in the one to one sessions. That doesn't have to wait until the end of the year either. It is much more relevant if a secondment to a project is coming up, that it should be discussed in a one to one. If your direct report wants to do something with a talent that has been spotted and needs developing, why wait until the end of the year to talk about it. All these discussions should be dynamic, regular.......and essentially part of business as usual.

This is a simple, practical, easy, time saving device, which many CEOs I have recommended it to have found to be really helpful.

The emerging consensus is that the Annual Performance appraisal is a process that should be consigned to the dustbin of history.

The new way of managing performance for the 21st Century, is to be fleet of foot. Dynamic, informal, up to date...............and part of business as usual. Are you a Leader who can regularly answer the question in the heads of your direct reports "how am I doing?" These recommendations will deliver that for you, with minimum effort beyond what you do now. It purely adds performance coaching to the one to one process, and requires that you keep a written record.

SUMMARY POINTS :

- Are you thinking you can't easily find time for Annual Performance Appraisals – so this recommendation to increase regularity won't be practical for you?

- Consider the reason that you hate Annual Performance Appraisal so much is because they are conflict-ridden and don't work!

- Do you currently manage through using regular one to ones with your direct reports? If you don't – you should – how else to you keep abreast of action?

- Adding 5/10 minutes of "how am I doing?" feedback to your regular one to ones is a simple practical regular performance coaching tool

- Regular performance reviews every month are a way of saving you time – by never again needing to sit down for that time wasting 2 hour conversation, and filling in those dreaded Annual Performance Appraisal forms

YOUR ACTIONS :

- Consider consigning old fashioned conflict-ridden Annual Performance Appraisal processes to the dustbin of history

- Save time and better motivate your people through a regular informal and dynamic performance coaching system

9. MANAGING PERFORMANCE – IT'S ALL ABOUT LEADERSHIP

YOU CANNOT 'BULLY' YOUR WAY TO BETTER PERFORMANCE

"The best way to inspire people to superior performance, is to convince them, by everything you do and by your everyday attitude, that you are wholeheartedly supporting them." Harold S Geneen

"If your actions inspire others to dream more, learn more, do more and become more, you are a leader." John Quincy Adams

"Choose a job you like, and you will never work a day in your life." Confucius

"The best leaders.......almost without exception at every level, are master users of stories and symbols." Tom Peters

"If we did all the things we are capable of, we would literally astound ourselves." Thomas Alva Edison

"The true measure of the value of any business leader and manager, is performance." Brian Tracy

"The conventional definition of management, is getting things done through people, but real management is developing people through work." Hasan Abedi

Getting High Performance:

Is Fear still a prevalent tactic of Leaders in the 21st Century?

As a reader, you may believe that the use of fear and bullying is a rarity in the workforce of today. You would be wrong. Way wrong!!

Data would definitely tell us otherwise. A Glassdoor Survey of 2000 UK workers in May 2017 found that 43% of respondents had been subjected to disrespectful behaviour by the manager. It seems that many people have at least one bad boss horror story.........and it still holds true (as it has always done) that people do not leave Companies, they leave bad bosses.

I think most Executives I speak with would say that fear makes workers less productive..................yet in a 2013 survey of 1277 workers, 47% said that they felt actively threatened by their manager. This rose to 58% in the Retail sector, and 75% in the Civil Service.

A further piece of corroborative data comes from the Arbitration and Conciliation Service (ACAS), which says that bullying is a serious problem in British work-places. Data from 2015 illustrates the fact that ACAS received 20,000 calls related to workplace bullying and harassment in one year, and this pattern is ongoing.

I think you would agree that these are concerning statistics. Yet, I think that they are entirely believable. Anecdotally, because performance does improve in the short term, by putting people under pressure ....it is my belief that there are still those in Leadership roles (especially but not exclusively – middle managers), who think this is the answer to raising performance. What these Leaders fail to grasp, is that performance tails off in the medium term, and as trust is lost – other consequences emerge. Those who can get out for other jobs (always your best people), will leave. Whilst others, who cannot or will not leave, become resentful and uncooperative. In some cases, Leadership behaviour will cause initiative resistance, and some individuals will become the 'internal terrorists' who fight progress every step of the way.

I'm sure we have all encountered those extremely negative employees........and examination as to what made them like that, often reveals that inadequate Leadership behaviour caused the bad reaction in the first instance.

Surely, there has to be a better way to increase performance!!

<u>British Cycling – my conversation with Dave Brailsford</u>

I rarely use sporting examples in my speaking or writing. Sporting examples can sometimes carry lessons for business, but often twist on a sudden change in sporting fortune. The same can be said to be true of British Cycling. Nevertheless, I think this story I am about to tell you holds some relevant lessons which stand over time.

Whilst working for Asda, I had cause to meet up with Dave Brailsford, way back before some of the real successes of later years in British Cycling. At the time, Asda was building a new Supercentre in Manchester Eastlands, next to the then Commonwealth Games site (now Manchester City's Etihad stadium) and the Manchester Velodrome.

David Brailsford had heard about the cultural turn-around at Asda, and wanted to hear the story about Asda becoming the UK's No1 Best place to work in the Sunday Times Best Companies survey. I wanted to hear about what Dave Brailsford was doing with coaching the British Cycling team.

We duly met up, along with Dave's resident psychologist, Steve Peters, at the Manchester Eastlands supercentre. I talked them through the story of the key tenets of the cultural change that Asda was engaged in delivering. In response, I was given a 'cook's tour' of the Velodrome in Manchester, and the cultural change they were attempt-ing themselves. Dave explained to me that much of coaching in sport has traditionally been undertaken by coaches who bully the athlete into higher levels of perfor-mance. That bullying has involved comments about diet; effort in training; frequency of training; starting times each day; and many other factors. Dave Brailsford wanted to change that philosophy in British Cycling, since he knew it to be unsuccessful. He articulated his philosophy of 'all carrot and no stick', and hence his hiring of Dr Steve Peters to help athletes to psychologi-cally overcome their various 'hang-ups', and perform at their very best. Their joint belief was that every potential athlete was already motivated to be a winner, they just needed the environment to encourage them.

Many people I speak to about British Cycling, know all about Dave Brailsford's 1% improvements in kit and equipment, but far less know about the rejection of fear and bullying, in favour of encouragement and facilitation coaching. We all know the success that Dave Brailsford has achieved with a variety of personalities competing in British Cycling, both in the British Team and at Sky. It is no coincidence, that his very different philosophy has been impactful in the lives of a number of cycling athletes.

In my view, this approach is applicable to business. How you lead and how your people feel, is certainly material to performance. Are you a carrot or a stick type coach? What is the Leadership tone of your organisation?

Leaders need to take a lead on creating a Performance Management environment which fits the modern workplace

A C.I.P.D. Survey of 2016, of 629 HR professionals, revealed that Performance Management was one of the top two skills needed by organisations (the other one being People Management). Of the survey respondents citing Performance Management as a top requirement – 53% said that senior leaders current skills in their organisations were inadequate in this area.

I believe that there is a major need for Leaders to step up to the plate, in a way they have never done before. This skill does not come naturally, and Leaders need skills training on having effective coaching conversations. Bullying is clearly not the way to access sustainable high performance. Neither is an antiquated once per year 'stab' at talking about the subject of performance. Success comes from regular and effective performance coaching conversations.

Leaders need to be able to 'touch-base' with their direct reports, on a regular and informal basis. Employees need to know the answer to that question: "how am I doing?" on an ongoing basis.

Long Term high performance and modern 21st Century Leadership

The organisations that will win on productivity in the long term, are those that are able to develop a dynamic way of managing people's performance informally and regularly. Business is fast moving. Information is constantly at our fingertips. Trends are quick to get away from us, unless we are able to be agile Leaders. Our Performance Management process needs to be as 'fleet of foot', as the world of today in which we all operate. Speed and lightness of touch is of the essence in Performance Management.

For me, it is a question of a modern Leadership style. If you are close to your people: if you are an encourager; if you want to develop your people through the work they do; if you regularly give time to one to one coaching of your direct reports.........you will see results. Your direct reports will easily adapt and respond to regular and informal performance coaching.........which will become the way of working in the organisation. I believe that Leaders need to be 'Coaching Leaders'........not the classic 'Command and Control' Leaders of yesteryear.

SUMMARY POINTS :

- Did you realise how much fear there was in the 21st Century UK workforce?

- Do you believe that fear eventually cripples performance? (Do you still have some sneaky admiration for the principle that it does no harm?)

- Is there fear in your own workplace? Do some of your own managers actually secretly bully people? How would you know/find out?

- Can you develop and encourage your Leaders to be 'coaching Leaders'?

- Are you prepared to put time and effort into training the skillset of good coaching conversations?

YOUR ACTIONS :

- Choose a style of Leadership for your organisation which motivates and engages your people

- Ensure your other Leaders follow and live that pattern in the way they lead

- Train Coaching Conversational skills to ensure delivery of quality performance coaching in one to ones

10. THIS IS NOT A FAD : IT'S A SEISMIC SHIFT – WHAT IS YOUR REACTION?

WILL YOU LEAD A CHANGE IN PERFORMANCE MANAGEMENT IN YOUR OWN ORGANISATION?

"Selecting the right people, with the potential to excel, and then developing those people through coaching and mentoring process to achieve greatness, is the primary responsibility of leadership. Effective leaders know precisely when to coach, when to mentor and when to manage." Dr Rick Johnson

"I am convinced that nothing we do is more important than hiring and developing people. At the end of the day, you bet on people, not on strategies." Larry Bossidy

"When a team outgrows individual performance and learns team confidence, excellence becomes a reality." Joe Paterno

"The highest levels of performance come to people who are centred, intuitive, creative and reflective – people who know how to see a problem as an opportunity." Deepak Chopra

Why Performance Management Fails (C.I.P.D. Survey 2015)

In 2015, the C.I.P.D. published a survey about why Performance Management fails in so many organisations. I think I have covered many, if not all of the reasons in this book, but here they are in a list, as an 'aide memoire' for you:-

- An over heavy administrative process (everyone always criticises the Performance Appraisal documentation – usually with good cause)
- The process is far too infrequent (once per annum is equivalent to 'forever' in a fast moving business)
- Failing to deal with underperformance (there is a natural tendency for conflict avoidance)
- It is a process for managing failure (looking backwards constantly is wrong - when you need to look forward)
- Forced distribution is fundamentally flawed (managers will find ways to 'game' the system)
- Stars get lost in the process (it is equally important to push talent as deal with underperformance)

What are the drivers of great Performance Management?

Having looked at what causes Performance Management to fail, there are drivers which can help to make it succeed:-

- Leaders must lead Performance Management (there is a Leadership requirement to remove bullying and coach/encourage performance dynamically)

- <u>Great conversations need to happen frequently</u> (the use of monthly one to ones is a great vehicle to include dynamic feedback in the last 10 minutes)
- <u>Creating an environment where performance is endemic</u> (if your culture encourages high quality feedback – you will win through)
- <u>Employee commitment via shared purpose/values</u> (if employees are committed then neither they nor managers will duck those difficult conversations)
- <u>Keep it simple</u> (one of the best drivers for anything to succeed in business is to keep things simple – what could be simpler that giving performance coaching feedback in your regular one to ones?)

<u>Driving the Performance Management agenda – by explaining "what's in it for me?"</u>

I have always believed that the development of people in organisations should be under a philosophy of 'self-development'. In other words, your personal development should not be 'done for you', by a paternalistic organisation. This inevitably leads to dissatisfaction, and the criticism that the organisation has failed to meet your development 'needs'. It seems inevitable that personal 'needs' for development, under that type of provision, will always outstrip the company resources, or its ability to deliver.

Far better then, to encourage employees to develop themselves, because the 'boot is on the other foot'. In this present age, where developmental tools and knowledge are readily available via the internet........it is relatively easy for employees to acquire knowledge......

watch TED talks, read up on the latest ideas......listen to book summaries whilst driving etc. If historically, your people have experienced the Annual Appraisal 'tick box' meeting with their line manager, then they need to understand that approach has been fundamentally flawed...............and they now need to look to their own development.

"What's in it for me?" under a dynamic regular process, becomes 12 opportunities in the year to discuss what you are doing to develop yourself, and where you might need help from your line manager. I believe this is hugely motivational, and very different from the once per year process. I know so many people, working in a variety of organisations, who rarely get an opportunity to discuss these topics with their line management. Making it 'business as usual', is a huge leap forward in performance coaching.

If you are considering the change to regular dynamic reviews, don't forget to brief your people about 'what's in it for them'........because they won't necessarily 'get it' automatically. Educating people who have been used to old processes requires clear communication. Briefing through the organisation, with inspiration, can potentially be a game changer.

Fluidity is key today : we sit on the brink of the 4th Industrial Revolution

We all know that the 1st Industrial Revolution occurred because of the age of steam power in the 18th Century. Workers came out of cottage industries into the great textile factories, and work moved from hand to machine power.

The 2nd Industrial Revolution was a 20th Century transition from steam power to electricity, together with the coming of mass manufacturing (which commenced in the Ford Model T Factory in the U.S.A. with the first ever production line).

A 3rd Industrial Revolution began in the 1970's, with the beginnings of the information age. We have seen the development of electronics and information technology revolutionise all our lives (both domestically and in the workplace).

Many commentators believe that we are on the cusp of the 4th Industrial Revolution today. That is, the potential to fuse digital; physical and biological spheres. Technological breakthroughs in Artificial Intelligence; 3D printing; biotechnology and nanotechnology will give us the power to do things which were unimaginable even 10 years ago. Such technological leaps will destroy barriers to entry in so many industries, quicker than ever before, since economies of scale are no longer really relevant.

This 4th Industrial Revolution will mean that companies who are inflexible, and not 'fleet of foot' will fail or struggle to compete. An obvious inflexibility is the outmoded hated Annual Performance Appraisal process. Adaptability/agility and responsiveness have always been important........but they must take on an ever more critical importance as we move into the 4th Industrial age.

In a stable world, Annual Performance Appraisal was clunky and ineffective at best. Indeed, in 1957, a Harvard Business School Professor said that it would be better to assess your own performance than to submit to the unnatural once per annum 'head to head' Performance Appraisal with your line manager. We have been very slow to respond to that view.

Fluidity/agility is going to count more increasingly in the ever more dynamic global environment in which we all now operate. I believe that we have to adopt a regular; dynamic performance coaching process...............which reflects and capitalises on that changed environment.

<u>Even the Civil Service has adopted regular/informal performance feedback!!</u>

The regular TV re-runs of "Yes Minister", have given us all the view that the Civil Service is an outdated management bureaucracy.

However, it would appear that it is not just the likes of Microsoft; IBM; Google; Accenture and Deloitte who have adopted dynamic regular informal Performance Appraisal.

Traditionally, the Civil Service had big issues with its Performance Management system. Famously, there was a strike at the Inland Revenue when managers were asked to rank the performance of individuals in their teams.

The latest thinking on Performance Management at the Civil Service, is attempting to change the history............

where too much focus has been on the process......
rather than the quality of the coaching conversations.
The Civil Service now believes that it is much better to
recognise outperformance; deal with underperformance;
and discuss development in regular conversations.................than to rely on a process which only
happened once per year. They are going to look at the
'how' (behaviours/values) as well as the 'what' (objectives), and seem to be embracing current thinking on
great Performance Management.

If the Civil Service can be brave.........so can you!!

10 Top Tips for successful Performance Management I.E.S. Research 2012

In my last book 'Culture trumps Strategy', I included a
summary of the 2012 research, carried out by the Institute
for Employment Studies – which subsequently translated
into 10 top tips for successful Performance Management.

I believe that these kind of summaries are exactly what
CEOs and line managers are looking for when thinking
about this type of topic, and successful implementation.
I therefore make no apology for including this information again in this book! I hope the shorthand is helpful.

i. ## Position Performance Management in terms of managing performance all year round

- Regularity of review conversations is key
- Set out priorities in one to ones
- Give feedback on progress (both good and bad)

ii. <u>Prioritise motivating performance and development conversations for all employees</u>

- Performance Management is for everyone
- It's not just for poor performers
- Quality of one to one conversations is vital

iii. <u>Keep the system simple and stable</u>

- Make it easy to do – how hard can this be?
- Don't fiddle with the process
- Set objectives/give feedback/agree action

iv. <u>Technology can support but shouldn't drive process</u>

- Putting the simple format online may help
- The power is still in the quality of the conversations
- The mantra must be – make it easy

v. <u>Objective setting is about business alignment</u>

- Work priorities change – discuss and amend regularly
- Make sure people know what to do – latest
- Make sure priorities align to the big picture

vi. <u>Any link to pay needs to be simple and transparent</u>

- Yet again – keep it simple
- Summarise regularly how the individual is doing

vii. <u>Clarify and emphasise development actions</u>

- All employees (excellent/average/poor performers) should be having support conversations
- Development actions should be relevant to the individual, and to the overall organisation

viii. <u>Support Managers in dealing with persistent poor performers</u>

- Some employees 'play games' and do 'just enough' to survive until the next conversation
- Managers need to help to 'weed out' those playing the system

ix. <u>Clarify the rules of appraiser and appraise</u>

- Managers should conduct good one to one conversations regularly and make time for them
- Employees should come to the table well prepared to discuss their performance objectively

x. <u>Performance Management training should be given</u>

- The best organisations train their Managers in this key skill – holding quality coaching discussions

<u>What are you going to do about this clarion call to update you Performance Management process?</u>

If you have been dissatisfied with your Performance Management process, then now really is the time to take action. There is a real alternative today, which fits with the modern dynamic workplaces of the 21st Century. It has been pioneered by those organisations in the vanguard of progress, and results are encouraging.

Why would you resist dropping something so universally despised, and replace it with something both effective and motivational? I urge you to take that step........and I know you will not regret it.

SUMMARY POINTS:

- Annual Performance Appraisal fails in most workplaces..........if yours is one such..........you are certainly not alone!

- It is the role of the Leader to hold regular useful conversations with their direct reports. How else will they really know 'how they are doing'?

- Explain 'what's in this' for the employee, and their ongoing self-development – brief with inspiration – this is the key to buy-in.

- Fluid Performance Management conversations fit perfectly in a world of businesses, sat at the brink of the 4th Industrial Revolution.

YOUR ACTIONS :

- Choose to lead the change to regular/simple performance coaching conversations

- Be brave enough to abandon the old fashioned, useless and much despised Annual tick box Performance Appraisal

- Determine to join the vanguard of change and get greater performance from your people – whilst motivating and developing them at the same time!

CPSIA information can be obtained
at www.ICGtesting.com
Printed in the USA
BVHW03s1100111018
529884BV00001B/124/P